ANOTHER HELPING OF DRAMASTUFF

Custer & Hoose's
ANOTHER HELPING OF DRAMASTUFF
Scenes About This and That and Other Spiritual Matters

Jim Custer and Bob Hoose

KANSAS CITY, MO 64141

ANOTHER HELPING OF DRAMASTUFF
Copyright © 1997
By Jim Custer and Bob Hoose

Amateur performance(s) rights are granted when two copies of this work are purchased.
Because this is copyrighted material, it is illegal to copy this material by any means except under the conditions outlined in the current Lillenas Drama Catalog or contact:

Lillenas Drama
Copyright Permission Desk
P.O. Box 419527
Kansas City, MO 64141
    Fax: 1-816-753-4071; E-mail: drama&lillenas.com

All rights reserved.
Printed in the United States of America
Cover art by Kevin Williamson

Scripture quotations are from the *New American Standard Bible* (NASB), © 1960, 1962, 1963, 1968, 1971, 1972, 1973, 1975, 1977 by The Lockman Foundation. Used by permission.

Dedication

When you dedicate a book, you ask yourself, "OK, who has helped get this masterpiece to its final conclusion? Who was the inspiration?" As we contemplated that, one name came to mind . . .

Terri McCoy

a dear friend who had the concern to say, "That doesn't make any sense." Or, "It would be better if you . . ." She is a very creative, funny, objective editor—and an actress to boot. What more can you ask. Thanks, Terri. Your check's in the mail.

Custer & Hoose

Contents

Preface   9

THIS (Scenes About Family and Friends)

1. It Happens to Everyone   11
   Two friends talk about death and about being 40
   2 male

2. One for All, and All for One   16
   Friend says thanks for loving her to health
   3 female

3. The Wake-up Call   21
   Scene about cherishing those things that are important
   1 male, 1 female

4. Hands Off   25
   A first date with two interpretations with a positive lesson
   1 boy, 1 girl

5. Breaking the Chains   27
   Becoming a father and forgiving your father all in one day
   2 male, 1 female

THAT (Scenes About Family and Seasons)

6. Hope   32
   A dark night before Easter, but a young mother is full of hope
   1 male, 1 female, 1 girl

7. Guess Who's Coming to Dinner   35
   Relatives are coming for Christmas dinner—need we say more?
   1 male, 1 female, 1 boy

8. Fossils   39
   Flashbacks of Thanksgiving and things never said
   2 male, 2 female

AND OTHER SPIRITUAL MATTERS

9. What Is a Christian?   45
   On-the-street interviews with three different responses
   1 male, 1 boy, 1 girl

10. What's Next?   49
    Readers theatre piece asking, "Now that I'm a Christian, what's next?
    4 readers

11. Mac and Newt   54
    Being uncomfortable with death
    2 male

12. Who Is God?   58
    Four scenes asking, "Who is God?"
    1 male, 2 female, 1 boy, 1 girl

Preface

Hello again, Christian dramatists everywhere. Thank you for picking up and (hopefully) buying this, our latest collection of scenes and sketches. This is a book of comic and dramatic pieces, dealing with a number of subjects that are designed for both sexes and a variety of ages. How's that for a rather general description?

There's not really a central theme here except that all 12 sketches just cried, "Pick me, pick me!" Well, actually 11 sketches cried, "Pick me, pick me!" and one said, "Yeah OK, fine." But we are happy with all and hope you will be too.

Have fun. We love ya, man.

Custer & Hoose

THIS (Scenes About Family and Friends)

It Happens to Everyone

Performance Tips and Pointers: Straight-ahead scene with a lot of one-liners. This piece was written with the rhythm of *Seinfeld* in mind. Don't get the wrong idea, I'm not saying we're good enough to create a perfect *Seinfeld* piece, but hopefully we got their timing. Running time: 5 minutes.

Topic: Growing older and liking our lives here on earth

Scripture: Genesis 6:12; Philippians 3:20

Set: Basic, two chairs

Time: Afternoon

Characters:

> MARTY: *in his late 30s. He is the calming influence on* DARRYL. *He can also push his buttons.*
>
> DARRYL: *41 years old and sure he has one foot in the grave*

Good for Sermons On: Changes in our lives • Should we like earth so much? • The reality of death

Synopsis: Marty and Darryl have just finished running. Darryl thinks he's having a heart attack. It's only a pin that he left in his shirt. Darryl has been worrying a lot about dying now that he's in his 40s. He doesn't want to die. He likes it here. Does he like it too much? He won't get a straight answer from Marty.

(Scene opens with DARRYL sitting in a chair taking off his jogging shoes. His friend MARTY enters from the kitchen with a glass of water and a towel draped around his neck. They've just finished running together.)

MARTY: Ahhh—boy do I feel run out! I figure if I keep doing this I might lose these 10 pounds I . . .

DARRYL (*interrupting and a little panicked*): Where's your heart?

MARTY: What?

DARRYL: Your heart . . . your heart? I think I'm having a heart attack! (*Holding the right side of his chest*)

MARTY: It's probably just a little—

DARRYL: Your heart . . . where's your heart?

MARTY: Uh . . . it's (*standing straight*) I pledge allegiance to the flag of the United States . . . it's here. (*Covering his left side*) It's on the left.

DARRYL: The left. You sure it's not on the right?

MARTY: I'm tellin' ya—it's on the left.

DARRYL: Maybe mine shifted . . . you know, when we were running.

MARTY: I don't think your heart can shift.

DARRYL: Well, I've got a pain. Ooooo . . . (*Holding his right side*) It's real sharp. Oooo.

MARTY: Well, sit down. (DARRYL *sits down.* MARTY *comes over.*)

DARRYL: Oooo, it hurts. I'm . . . I'm short of breath.

MARTY: It's because you're short.

DARRYL: You sure?

MARTY: Now where does it hurt?

DARRYL: What do you mean, where does it hurt? You're not a doctor.

MARTY: I took first aid. At the office we had to take first aid . . . in case anyone did something where they needed . . . first aid. Let me see. Now where?

DARRYL: Here. (DARRYL *points, and every time he hits his chest he yelps in pain.*) Oooo, here, ooo, here! It's like a knife cutting right through me.

MARTY (MARTY *looks and touches him*): Here?

DARRYL: Ooowww!

MARTY (*finding something sticking through his shirt*): It's a pin! You forgot to take a tag off that had a pin in it.

DARRYL: Oh. (*Taking out the tag*) I bought this yesterday. I guess I forgot to get all the pins out. But it could'a been a heart attack.

MARTY: Yeah—if you were backward. You're nuts.

DARRYL: I'm not nuts. You'll find out when you turn 40. Something happens—death becomes a reality.

MARTY: Death is a reality every night when Angie cooks dinner.

DARRYL: You refuse to take me seriously. *(Beat)* Ted . . . what's his name?

MARTY: Kennedy?

DARRYL: No . . . no . . . the guy that lives . . . used to live down the street. Ted! Ted!

MARTY: Roosevelt.

DARRYL *(incredulous):* Roosevelt . . . Kennedy. Did you know a Ted Roosevelt that lived down . . . *(Remembering)* Adams! Ted Adams went jogging last spring and boom! He was dead. 41 and boom! What do you say to that?

MARTY: He had a bad heart.

DARRYL: He was 41! I'm 41! I could have a bad heart—or a bad kidney, bad liver, bad—

MARTY: Breath.

DARRYL *(miffed):* Breath. Always with the jokes. I pour my soul out to ya, and you make jokes.

MARTY: You're making too much of this, Darryl. You're fine; you're strong as an ox.

DARRYL: That's probably what they said to Ted . . . just before . . . boom. *(Beat)* I don't know, Marty . . . it's all I think about anymore. I hear reports on television . . . ya know. How heart disease is getting this many and cancer is getting that many and . . . I don't know. I mean, he was 41!

MARTY: Yeah, but George Burns lived to be 100. He had three martinis a day, smoked cigars, and he lived to be 100.

DARRYL: He was Jewish.

MARTY: What does that have to do with it?

DARRYL: They're God's chosen people.

MARTY: So?

DARRYL: So He likes them better than us.

MARTY: You're nuts.

DARRYL: I'm not nuts. *(Starts to stand, then as he speaks he grabs his head.)* Oww . . . my head. I'm dizzy.

MARTY: You stood up too soon. Sit down.

DARRYL: Could be a brain tumor . . . you don't know.

MARTY: That would require a brain. You're becoming obsessive.

DARRYL: I know. I'm turning into my mother.

MARTY: Does your wife know?

DARRYL: This is how she was. Always some pain or illness. She was a . . . *(thinking)* a hypodermic.

MARTY: Hypochondriac.

DARRYL: Whatever. It's happening to me. It was crossing the big 4-0. You haven't crossed it yet, so you don't know. But it's like everything changed. Things get . . . "iffy."

MARTY: Iffy?

DARRYL: Yeah. The eyesight's a little iffy . . . my hair's a little iffy . . . my waist is a little iffy . . .

MARTY: No . . . your waist is a definite . . . it blends into your lap. Your lap is iffy.

DARRYL: You're doing it again. I'm being serious—you're being Don Rickles.

MARTY: I'm just trying to get you to lighten up.

DARRYL: I can't lighten up. OK . . . OK . . . the other day I noticed I lost my sense of smell. I don't smell, Marty. I don't smell.

MARTY: Believe me, you smell.

DARRYL *(not catching it):* No. I don't smell. These are the kinds of changes. You don't know. You haven't turned 40. But you will . . . then you'll know. I started thinking about death, ya know. I mean, it never entered my mind at 20 or 30 . . . but 40 . . . surprise. People die in their 40s.

MARTY: People die in their 20s too. And 60s, 80s . . .

DARRYL: But I don't want to die. I like it here. Is that wrong? To like it here? I mean, do you think the Lord gets offended when we say we like it here?

MARTY: I doubt it.

DARRYL: 'Cause I don't want to offend Him. You know, He went to prepare a place for us . . . a real nice place . . . I don't want Him to think I'm standing here . . . *(catching himself)* sitting here and saying . . . "Aaaa, keep it." That wouldn't be right. I want to go there . . . someday. Just not today.

MARTY: I wouldn't worry about it. When it's time . . . you'll go.

DARRYL *(thinking):* Yeah. Happens to everyone.

MARTY: Some sooner than others.

DARRYL: Ah . . . why'd ya have to go and say that!

MARTY: Come on. You've got years ahead. You're young. You're in the prime of your life.

DARRYL: You think so?

MARTY: Sure. Besides, I don't think the Lord is so crazy about having you up there yet. He's already busy dealing with your mother.

DARRYL: Oh, you're right. He probably needs a few more years to get my place ready, anyway.

MARTY: Of course. A nice little place way out in the country. I guess we're stuck with you.

DARRYL: I'm feeling better.

MARTY: Good. You look better. *(Beat)* Except for that . . . mole on the side of your neck. Have you had that checked lately?

DARRYL *(panicked):* Mole! What mole? *(He runs off to look.)*

MARTY *(smiles):* Too easy—just too easy. *(He exits.)*

One for All, and All for One

Performance Tips and Pointers: This scene takes place in an airplane, so whatever you can do to cement that idea from the beginning would be good. You can stage it with the three women sitting next to each other and another row of people beside or behind them as you would find in an airplane. Start the scene with "California, Here I Come." Running time: 6 minutes.

Topic: Loving each other through the tough times

Scripture: Proverbs 17:7

Set: An airplane. You will need "touristy" costumes, candy bars.

Time: Midday

Characters:

VIOLET: *a woman in her 50s who is very tender and soft-spoken. She comes off sometimes as a little airheaded.*

DOROTHY: *a woman also in her 50s. She tends to be a bull in a china closet. Definitely the outspoken leader of the trio.*

GLADYS: *a woman in her 50s who is a former beauty queen. She thinks she still has the stuff to attract any man. She and Dorothy have one of those competitive relationships that can make things a little edgy.*

V.O.: *a pilot's voice*

Good for Sermons On: Accountability ● Friendship ● Supporting each other in the hard times

Synopsis: Violet is taking Dorothy and Gladys on a surprise vacation. It's been a tough year for Violet and her husband. Little did the other ladies know that they were loving Violet to health. This little vacation was just a way of saying "thanks."

(Scene opens in the dark. We hear the sound of a jet taking off. Lights come up on three ladies sitting close to each other in the same row. They are in an airplane.)

V.O.: Now that we've achieved our cruising altitude, ladies and gentlemen, please sit back and enjoy your flight. Our trip to Los Angeles [or other appropriate destination] should take us approximately 2 hours and 50 minutes.

VIOLET: Oh, I just can't wait to get there. I'm so excited.

DOROTHY: We are, too, honey.

GLADYS: I didn't mention it when we walked in because they were so rudely pushing us into our seats, but did you see that gray-haired man in first class when we came on board?

DOROTHY *(gives GLADYS a look):* They were pushing you to sit down because you were plugging up the whole aisle. People couldn't get to their seats.

GLADYS: Dorothy! I was not "plugging up" anything. I just got a little stuck, that's all.

DOROTHY: A little stuck? Uh-huh. Between you and those 15,000 bags of yours, you were wedged in so tight it took three attendants, the pilot, and a tube of Vaseline to break you free.

VIOLET: I was a little worried, Gladys.

GLADYS: Oh, that's nonsense, I only have 5 bags, and I just got a wee bit tangled up for a few seconds. Besides, I need all those things on this trip. I like to be prepared when I travel.

DOROTHY: Well, good. I'd say you're prepared now to change clothes every half hour.

GLADYS: I'll have you know that there are more than just clothes in those bags. I brought makeup, books, food, first-aid supplies . . .

VIOLET: You brought food? Gladys, honey, we can buy food in Los Angeles.

GLADYS: Well, it's not food exactly.

DOROTHY: What exactly is it?

GLADYS: Uh—energy bars.

DOROTHY: Candy bars. You brought a suitcase full of candy bars?

GLADYS: I did not fill a suitcase full of candy. *(Beat)* Just my purse.

VIOLET: Oh, my.

GLADYS: Anyway, I don't want to talk about my luggage. Did you see that handsome gray-haired man in first class. *(She looks up the aisle to see if she can spot him.)* I bumped into him, and he winked at me. Looks like I still have the gift, ladies.

DOROTHY: Mmm, perhaps you should open it up and find out what it is. *(Beat)* He winked at you?

GLADYS: He most certainly did, and then he fell to his knees to politely help me look for any of my belongings that might have fallen out of my bag.

VIOLET: I don't think he was winking. I think he was blinking back tears.

GLADYS: What?

DOROTHY: Well, you hit him full in the face with that big bag. It's a wonder if you didn't break his nose.

GLADYS: Dorothy!

DOROTHY: And after he slumped to the floor, he was groping around for his front teeth.

VIOLET: I'm sure he'll be all right. He looked healthy. It's just a shame to mar his looks like that.

GLADYS *(pauses as she looks at her friends)*: Well, now you've upset me.

DOROTHY: Oh, come on.

GLADYS: No, I'm serious. The two of you have already ruined this weekend for me. I should never have come. I don't even know why you invited me in the first place.

VIOLET: I had to invite you, honey. You were the reason I wanted to take this trip. You're the guest of honor. You and Dorothy both.

GLADYS: What?

VIOLET: Well, I wanted to wait till we landed, but I suppose this is as good a time as any to explain.

DOROTHY: Good. I've been on pins and needles waiting to find out what this big splurge on your part was all about. I hate secrets, especially when I can't spill them to someone else.

VIOLET: OK. *(Takes a deep breath and gathers her words)* The two of you mean so much to me. I'm not sure where I'd be without you. *(Beat)* You've support-ed me, you've held me accountable, you're two beautiful women who have been my rock in stormy weather . . .

GLADYS *(petulant)*: Now, Violet, if you're saying this just to make me feel better, well, it's not necessary.

DOROTHY: Be quiet, Gladys. I like it. *(Sweetly)* Go on, Violet.

VIOLET: Well, first a little history. *(Beat)* This is hard. You probably aren't aware of just how bad things were between Jack and I. I kept it pretty hidden. After 20 years . . . well, I felt like such a loser. It was so frightening. We were fighting like cats and dogs. The slightest word could erupt into a screaming battle. So we stopped talking. We slept in separate rooms; we even started eating our meals apart. I'd put dinner on the table for Jack; then I'd eat in the kitchen. The house was like a tomb. Everything that was once alive had died.

DOROTHY *(tries to throw in a joke):* Sounds normal. *(She realizes just how serious* VIOLET *is.)* I'm sorry. Me and my mouth sometimes. *(Touches* VIOLET's *hand)* Go ahead, please.

GLADYS: Wait. We didn't know any of this. I didn't help at all. If I'd known, I could've . . .

VIOLET: That's just the point. You didn't know, so what you both did for me wasn't out of sympathy. You loved me back to life again because you actually loved me. *(Beat)* Dorothy, you always made me laugh when I felt least like it. Gladys, you always sensed my pity parties coming on and kicked me in the behind to get out of it. *(To both)* And all the while, when you saw me at my weakest and you couldn't figure me out (goodness, I couldn't figure myself out), you both encouraged me to look to my faith in God, to recognize what was really of value, really important. There was a point when I thought I had no faith left, till you made it real again. *(Beat, realizing)* What I guess I mean is—you were God's love to me.

(GLADYS *and* DOROTHY *are both quiet for a moment as the weight of this sinks in.)*

DOROTHY: Violet, honey, that's the sweetest thing anyone's ever said to me. Why, I feel downright holy.

GLADYS: Are you and Jack . . . ?

VIOLET: We're better now. We stuck it out. We've been going to counseling. It's not perfect, but it's better.

GLADYS: Perfect, hah! Nothing on this earth is perfect, except maybe chocolate —and Mel Gibson.

DOROTHY: Forget it, Gladys, both of them are too rich for your waistline.

GLADYS: Dorothy!

VIOLET: See, this is what I mean. The two of you are wonderful. How can I think of myself as a loser when I'm around you two?

GLADYS: I'm not sure how to take that.

VIOLET: Anyway, that's why I dipped into savings for this trip. Since Jack and I just made it through a good year together, I figured I owed you two a celebration. Jack thought so too. So he took your husbands hunting, and I got you.

DOROTHY: You got the better end of the deal, believe me.

GLADYS: So here we are. The Three Musketeers winging our way in comfort to the City of Angels.

DOROTHY (*smiles*): Hmmm.

VIOLET (*awkward pause*): Except for these seats. I swear they make these seats for anorexic dwarfs. And if this joker in front of me leans his chair back any farther, I'll be able to rest my chin on his forehead.

GLADYS and DOROTHY: Violet!

VIOLET: Just joking. I had to clear the air with a little griping. Things were getting too nice. (*They all laugh.*)

DOROTHY: Thank you for all this. We love you.

VIOLET (*she grabs their hands*): I love you musketeers too.

DOROTHY: Hey, speaking of musketeers, this is supposed to be a celebration, isn't it? OK, Gladys. Grab your purse and break out the "energy bars."

(GLADYS *hands them each a candy bar. They raise them in the sky like crossed swords.*)

VIOLET: On to Los Angeles.

GLADYS: And Mel.

DOROTHY: Here, here.

Blackout

The Wake-up Call

Performance Tips and Pointers: This scene is a very poignant piece that should be done very deliberately. You can be as elaborate as you want with the set. The lighting should be warm. Start the scene with a short musical interlude. Then, when Harry takes Angie's hand and she kneels beside him, bring in some underscoring that will set that moment apart. That moment is key to the success of the scene, so take your time. Running time: 5 to 6 minutes.

Topic: Taking time to love your family

Scripture: Luke 12:34

Set: Living room; a chair, pictures

Time: Late afternoon

Characters:

HARRY: *a man in his middle to late 40s. He is troubled by a recent heart attack that caught him off guard and forced him to evaluate his priorities.*

EVELYN: *his wife. She is a few years younger than Harry and is a little too protective but yet patient.*

ANGIE: *their 16- or 17-year-old daughter*

Good for Sermons On: The priorities of life ● Family ● Taking time to see the life around you

Synopsis: Harry had a mild heart attack that is beginning to cause a change in his life. He realizes he doesn't remember some special times of the past. It isn't the heart attack that caused the problem, it's that he was too busy to take the time to notice. The heart attack was a wake-up call to cherish those things that are really important.

(*Scene opens with* HARRY *sitting in a chair center stage.*)

EVELYN: Harry. Harry?

HARRY (*snaps out of his reverie*): Oh. Yeah—just . . .

EVELYN: Are you all right? I've been calling.

HARRY: Fine, I'm fine . . . just thinking . . . I'm fine.

EVELYN (*a little concerned*): Are you having chest pains again? You don't look well.

HARRY (*a little defensive*): No, really, I'm fine. What did you need?

EVELYN (*coming closer*): Sweetheart, you've been looking poorly all day. Are you sure you're all right?

HARRY (*firmly*): Evelyn! I'm fine, for pity's sake. I had a slight heart attack—not a stroke. I don't need a nursemaid checking my pulse every two minutes! (EVELYN *is stung by his words and just stares at him in silence. Just before she leaves in tears,* HARRY *realizes his blunder.*) Look, honey, I'm sorry. That was uncalled for. It's—it's just . . . the stress of these . . . changes, I guess. I'm sorry.

EVELYN (*still stung but recovering*): The last thing you're supposed to be dealing with is stress. Why don't you talk to me about this?

HARRY (*pause, rubs his face in resignation*): I don't know, honey. I'm not . . . even sure what I can tell you. It's just . . . I don't know.

EVELYN (*touches him*): Harry—we're here to help. We love you.

HARRY: I know.

EVELYN: Then what's going on up here, huh? (*Touches his head*) What is it? The doctor said you'd be able to do just about everything you could before. We've got to change your diet a bit, and get a little more exercise, but it'll all turn out fine. You'll see.

HARRY (*he smiles then picks a picture off his lap*): Do you remember this?

EVELYN: Do I remember it?

HARRY: Yes. What is it?

EVELYN: It's our family portrait. So what—?

HARRY: Do you remember what happened that day?

EVELYN: What?

HARRY: What happened before we took that picture?

EVELYN (*looks at him with a "where is this going?" look*): Nothing. (HARRY *won't let it go.*) All right. Uh, I just picked Angie up from preschool. (*Remembering*) That was the day of her school fair, as I remember. In fact, she brought home that darling little horse that she made out of seashells; you said it looked like a cockroach, remember? You got home early, we went to the studio, then stopped for an early dinner so you could get to your meeting in time. Like I said, nothing.

22

HARRY *(sighs)*: Therein lies the tale.

EVELYN: What?

HARRY: I can't remember a bit of it.

EVELYN: Well—it was over 10 years ago.

HARRY: You remembered.

EVELYN: I'm a woman.

HARRY: The point is, I don't remember anything. I was sitting here looking at this. I don't even remember Angie at five, nonetheless her seashell animal. I closed my eyes and had a hard time remembering her face now, even though I had breakfast with her this morning.

EVELYN: What are you saying? I've never heard of memory loss with a heart attack.

HARRY: No, no. You can't lose what you never had. I'm sitting here trying to remember—anything. It's like I've been absent from life for the last 20 years. At least your lives.

EVELYN: Now don't upset yourself, Harry. It's not going to help anything.

HARRY: Don't you see, Ev. This is a wake-up call, that's what it is. For the first 10 years of our marriage, I put every heartbeat into a firm that bumped me out with the first layoff. And in spite of that, I turned around and slapped the shackles on again, and I've made the same stupid mistakes ever since. But then BAMMO! Heart attack, slam on the brakes. And today it hit me. Why didn't I die? It's because it's wake-up-buddy-kick-ya-in-the-pants-scales-off-the-eyes time. It's God's warning, that's what this is. *(Beat)* And so I've decided . . . I'm done with it. I'm quitting the rat race. Come Monday, I resign. I'm through.

EVELYN: Harry, you're scaring me. Look. I'm not saying I haven't wanted changes. I have. I want more than anything for us to pull close and be a team together, which I think is what you're saying too. But let's not throw the baby out with the bath water. I don't think God wants you to toss out everything you've worked for.

HARRY: I've got to do something, Ev. I'm losing you and Angie. I know it—day by day. I've been making the choice to bail out on you, Angie, and God.

EVELYN: All right, all right—just take it step by step. Take the time. You've earned that. Let's all work together, a day at a time. OK? *(Touches him)* This is good.

(ANGIE *enters.)*

ANGIE: Mom, Dad, I'm home and I've got . . . is everything OK?

EVELYN: Sure, everything's fine. *(She squeezes* HARRY's *hand and gets up.)* I'll have dinner ready in a few minutes. (HARRY *smiles at her.*)

ANGIE: Great, I'm starved. (EVELYN *exits.*) Can I get you something, Dad?

HARRY: No, no, I'm fine.

ANGIE: OK. *(Starts to exit)*

HARRY: Angie, wait.

ANGIE *(stops):* Huh?

(HARRY *takes her hand and gently pulls her down. She kneels beside him. He just looks at her, searching her face, taking the time to memorize what she looks like. After a brief pause, he smiles.)*

ANGIE: What is it?

HARRY: Nothing. *(Starts getting up)* Why don't I walk in with you. You can help your feeble old man find his place at the table.

ANGIE: Yeah, right. *(She puts her arm around her dad.)*

HARRY *(as they exit):* You're growing into quite a lovely young lady, aren't you?

ANGIE *(embarrassed):* Dad!

(They exit.)

Hands Off

Performance Tips and Pointers: A very simple scene to be done straight ahead with your two young actors. This sketch is written for older junior high or younger adolescent kids. It has a very fast pace that would point up the contrast in how each saw the evening's date. You will need to talk to your youth about certain lingo. Please feel free to change some of the words to fit the current dialogue of the day. Running time: 1 to 1½ minutes.

Topic: Integrity

Set: Either to be done with the actors standing in two separate spots or sitting on bar stools

Time: Anytime

Characters:
BOY: *just that; about 14*
GIRL: *definitely; about 13*

Good for Sermons On: Integrity ● Relationships ● Dating

Synopsis: It was a very anticipated date that turned out pretty well. Granted, there was a difference in how the events of the date were interpreted, but a very valuable lesson was still learned.

(Scene opens with BOY *and* GIRL *standing or sitting on bar stools on opposite sides of the stage in solo spots. Dialogue goes back and forth between them as they tell us their different versions of the same story.)*

BOY: This girl was a "babe," ya know? I was thinkin' we're gonna have fun tonight. I mean, my socks were meltin'!

GIRL: I thought he was cute. He sorta looks like Jonathan Taylor-Thomas, and he's fine! So when he asked me to go to the movies with him, how could I say no?

BOY: So, we're walking over to the movies—right. My lips are telling me, "Go get her, boy." But I'm thinking, "I gotta be cool."

25

GIRL: We got to the movies, and he was so nice. He bought me candy and Coke and everything.

BOY: Loosen her up with the sweets, you know? Two things girls can't resist— sugar and my love.

GIRL: He put his arm around me but didn't try anything like some other jerks would have. He even cried during the movies. He's so sensitive.

BOY: I started makin' my move, ya know—slip the old arm around her shoulder, but then this really groady scene happened in the movie. So, by the time I started thinking about, well, ya know, I couldn't find it, my hand, I mean! My whole arm was asleep. It hurt like a "mama chicken." Brought tears to my eyes.

GIRL: He walked me back to my front door. He was real quiet. He looked so cute and shy with his hands in his pockets. I just had to kiss him on the cheek—good-night.

BOY: We're walking back to her house. She's talking, but I'm thinking, "Man! The night's almost over, and I haven't made my move. She's gonna think I'm weird." Then, I realize that my breath smelled like week-old popcorn and butter substitute. I'm goin' through my pockets for some gum and BAMMO! She kisses me on the cheek. I sorta went, "Uh . . . ," which sounded real cool. She thanks me for being a perfect gentleman and goes inside.

GIRL: I watched him through the window, and he just stood there for the longest time with this cute grin on his face. Then he went home. He's even cooler than Jonathan Taylor-Thomas. He's . . . *(Pause)* I like him.

BOY: She said I was a perfect gentleman. I'd never been a perfect gentleman before. *(Pause and thinks)* Cool!

Blackout

Breaking the Chains

Performance Tips and Pointers: This scene could open with hospital sounds. The set can be as simple or as elaborate as you would like it to be. Clearly define your entrances and exits. Part of the power of this scene will be when Sam looks at where his father went then moves to the "delivery room." If you want some underscoring, I would start it after the Nurse's line, "She has your eyes." Running time: 8 to 9 minutes.

Topic: The thing that influences our children is our own character. Breaking generational sin.

Scripture: Ephesians 6:4

Set: Waiting room in a hospital outside the delivery room. (Optional) Chairs, coffeemaker, trash can, hospital sounds.

Time: Anytime. Evening or early morning might be better.

Characters:
> NURSE: *a woman that can be any age. She has a great sense of humor.*
> SAM: *a man in his middle 20s. He has a weak stomach for anything that might involve blood.*
> JAKE: *a man in his middle to late 40s that looks much older. He has had a rough life. There is a gentleness in his spirit.*
> MAN: *nonspeaking*

Good for Sermons On: Reaping what we sow • Raising children, a parents legacy • Breaking the bad patterns of generations • Fathers and sons

Synopsis: Sam has had a tough time as his wife is giving birth. He is forced to leave. His father comes to see if he is all right. There is very little relationship between Sam and his father, Jake. Jake is a recovering alcoholic and is trying his best to bridge the gap between him and his son. It's tough, but he leaves his son with something important to think about.

(Scene opens in a hospital waiting room. There is no one here for a few seconds; then a young man in his 20s comes in, dressed in hospital scrubs and being helped by a nurse, who is also dressed in scrubs.)

NURSE *(holding up* SAM): You're about there. *(Pulling up a chair with her feet as she continues to hold up* SAM. *Then she plops him in the chair.)* Now put your head between your knees.

SAM *(raising his head):* But I should . . .

NURSE *(pushing his head between his knees):* Between the knees.

SAM *(raising his head again):* But she is my wife . . . and I am her husband.

NURSE *(pushing his head back down):* I'll remember that when we do the birth certificate . . . between the knees.

SAM: But . . .

NURSE: You're too heavy for me to carry out again.

SAM: She needs me.

NURSE: No offense, Mr. Randolf, but you were of no use on the floor. She'll be fine.

SAM: It was the screaming.

NURSE: I told you to stop. You yell like that and you lose oxygen. Just stay here, and I'll come back when it's over. You're gonna be a father.

SAM: You don't think the child will feel slighted, do you? I mean, not seeing its father when it comes out of the . . . *(Starting to get squeamish as he tries to say the word "womb")*

NURSE *(pushing his head back down):* Don't think about it. I'm sure the child will have enough on its mind . . . you know, breathing . . . things like that.

SAM: I just don't want any regressed memories 20 years from now.

NURSE: I understand. *(Starts to leave)* I'll be back.

SAM: Nurse . . . I really am a man, you know, strong, macho . . .

NURSE: I'm sure you are. If you need to throw up or . . .

SAM *(interrupting):* Oh, please, don't say . . .

NURSE: In case—a trash can is right beside you.

(SAM, *with his head between his knees, waves to her then reaches over for the trash can and puts it under his head. She exits with a smile. After a few seconds, a man in his 40s, who looks much older, comes in, looks around as if he's looking for someone. He is wearing a raincoat and hat. He walks around, then notices* SAM. SAM *raises his head and takes a deep breath. He then notices the man. His reaction is subdued.)*

JAKE: Son . . . *(Catching himself)* Sam. Is everything all right?

SAM *(a little reluctant):* Yeah. *(Self-consciously moving the trash can away so as not to appear weak)*

JAKE: I mean with Beth.

SAM: Yeah—she's fine.

JAKE (*awkward moment*): Uh—mind if I sit?

(SAM *at first doesn't say anything; just thinks, "I suppose it's OK." There is another pause.*)

SAM: How did you know?

JAKE: Your sister called.

SAM (*not looking at him*): How'd she know where to find you?

JAKE (*getting up to take off his coat and hat*): Oh . . . I uh . . . I'm living in some . . . housing on Blake. It's not the Taj Mahal, but it's OK. I . . . uh . . . I've seen her . . . a coupl'a times. She and her kids came over. That little one sure looks like you when you were that age. (*Short pause*) I've . . . I've stopped drinking.

SAM (*looking at him, skeptical*): How long this time? (*Awkward pause*) Listen, I think . . . uh . . . everything's gonna be all right, so you don't have to . . .

JAKE (*about to have his coat hung up when he notices what* SAM *is about to say*): Oh . . . yeah . . . well, I'll just call your sister. She was a little worried. She just want-ed me to check on you. Their driveway was flooded. Couldn't get out. Rain-ing cats and dogs out there. You're OK?

SAM: I'm . . . I'm OK.

JAKE: OK. Mind if I get some coffee . . . before I go?

SAM: No.

JAKE (*moving over to the coffeepot*): I've been going to AA. We're learning to take one day at a time. Look, I don't expect you to believe me. I know I've said this sorta thing before, but I was hoping we could, you know.

SAM: I don't . . .

(*He turns to say something caustic when the* NURSE *comes in helping another man to a couch.*)

NURSE: Must be an epidemic. (*To* SAM) You doing OK?

SAM: Yeah.

NURSE (*noticing* JAKE): Friend?

SAM (*not knowing what to say*): Uh . . .

JAKE: I'm Jake.

NURSE: Here to give a little moral support, huh? Good. Ever since women's lib . . . they've been dropping like flies.

(NURSE *points to the guy she just brought in who has his head between his legs.*)

NURSE (*to* JAKE): Keep an eye on that one too. (*She exits.*)

JAKE (*to* SAM): Want some coffee?

SAM: Just a little.

JAKE (*pouring coffee*): I remember when you were born. Your mother was fine. I was the one who couldn't handle the pressure. I was fixing this nursery up—in the old washroom. You know, painting, building some shelves— she comes in and tells me her water broke. I panicked. Even though we'd talked about what we were going to do—you know running through the routine—I just fritzed out. All I could think about was "her water broke," so I grabbed my tool box instead of the suitcase we'd packed. She laughed so hard I thought she was going to give birth in the car. Kept saying, "Jake, the crescent wrench isn't gonna fix this one." (*He lightly laughs.*)

SAM (*taking coffee from* JAKE): Thanks.

JAKE: Then when we got to the hospital—I just kept drinking.

(SAM *looks at him like "I bet you did."*)

JAKE (*noticing*): Coffee—and pacing back and forth. They said I could go in, but I declined. I wanted to be there, but—well—I get nauseous trimming my toenails. After you were born they told me I could see you. Your—your mother had a smile on her face from ear to ear. She said, "Come over here and hold your son, Samuel. He has your eyes." She always liked my eyes. Said they reminded her of James Dean. (*Laughs a little*) I don't know. (*Awkward pause*) What are you going to name—?

SAM: Not sure. Beth . . . Beth has a thing for names. She's convinced what you name a child helps determine who they'll become.

JAKE: Maybe she's right. (*Pause*) Sam . . . I know advice coming from me isn't . . . well, I have no right, but I've . . . since I've stopped drinking, I've stopped a lot of things, time mainly . . . to think.

SAM: Look, I don't know if I'm in any condition to have this conversation right now.

JAKE: It's not a name that shapes a child, but what the child sees in you—the parent. I didn't realize that, or if I did, I didn't allow myself to acknowledge it. I guess it was spending time with your sister's kids. They're so— so good, so much like your sister. I'm sorry—

SAM: You don't have to say—

JAKE (*interrupting*): Yes, I do. I'm sorry I wasn't there. I'm sorry I didn't give you something to be proud of. If I could do it all over again, I would do it differently.

SAM: It's—it's a little late for that.

JAKE: I know. *(Uncomfortable)* Well—I'd better go. *(Starts to walk out, then turns)* Sam, don't get so—so distracted that you don't take the time and ask yourself, "What do I want my child to see in me?" Take care.

(JAKE exits. SAM watches him go, thinks. Then the NURSE comes in with a big smile on her face.)

NURSE: Well—you're a father.

SAM *(excited):* I am! Of what?

NURSE: A six-pound cocker spaniel.

SAM: Huh?

NURSE: A six-pound baby girl.

SAM: A girl?

NURSE: Yep. Checked the plumbing myself.

SAM: How's Beth?

NURSE: Well, she's not ready for the New York Marathon, but she's all right. She said she forgave you for putting her through this.

SAM *(laughs):* Can I see her? Both of them?

NURSE: Sure, room 3.

SAM: I'm a father.

NURSE: It gets better. *(Starts to exit, then turns)* She's a lucky little girl—she has your eyes. *(She exits.)*

(SAM thinks for a moment, looks over his shoulder where JAKE exited; then he moves to the delivery room.)

THAT (Scenes About Family and Seasons)

Hope

Performance Tips and Pointers: Scene should be done in a tight spot. It should open with sirens in the background, perhaps a flashing red light offstage giving us the effect of police and a fire truck nearby. The woman takes a cup as the light comes on. She is talking to an imaginary person, but we must feel that she is there. When the fireman comes in, he should be in the dark out of the spot with his back to the audience. While coaching your actress, please have her ask the questions the person is asking her, in her own mind, before responding. Approximate running time: 4 minutes.

Topic: Easter is a time for hope

Scripture: Titus 3:1-7 (especially verse 7)

Set: Outside a house, sitting on a curb. A cup, blanket, old Bible.

Time: Sometime in the evening

Characters:
> MOTHER: *a woman in her 30s*
> GIRL: *her daughter, about 6 or 7*
> FIREMAN: *exactly that*

Good for Sermons On: The hope of Easter ● The night before Easter being very dark ● Praying for your loved ones

Synopsis: There has been a fire and a young, divorced mother (with her daughter) is sitting outside their home wrapped in a blanket. Everything they owned has gone up in smoke. A lady has brought her a cup of something to drink. In the course of their discussion, we find out that the young mother has been away from the Lord, but her mother never stopped praying for her. She has been going through a rebirth in her thinking. She has started going back to church. She has found people who care. It is the dark night before Easter, but the young mother is full of hope.

(Scene is done in a tight spot. A MOTHER *is sitting with a small* GIRL, *both are wrapped in a blanket. They have black smudges on their faces as if they've been through a fire, which is exactly what they've been through.)*

MOTHER *(reaching as if someone has just given her a cup with something to drink):* Thank you. *(To the young* GIRL*)* Here, honey, the nice lady gave us something to drink. (GIRL *takes a sip. To the person who has handed her the drink.)* Thanks.

GIRL: Mommy. What about my Easter eggs?

MOTHER: Well . . . *(Looking over her shoulder to where her house once was)* Maybe your daddy can help you get some more. It'll be OK.

GIRL: But I won't have a basket.

MOTHER *(to the other person):* Huh? Well—thank you, you're very kind. *(To the* GIRL*)* The nice lady says you can have one of hers. *(To the other person)* She's going to her cousin's house tomorrow for an Easter egg hunt. She's been looking forward to it for weeks. We spent all last night coloring eggs. They weren't masterpieces but . . . *(looking over her shoulder)*, but I wish we hadn't lost them. *(Trying to put a happy face on the situation)* Oh well . . . *(Pause)* I'm not sure. Probably wiring or something. I'm just not sure. The fireman said it would be easy to track down. I . . . I just hope I didn't do something . . . you know . . . wrong. Ever since Jack and I divorced . . . I . . . well I . . . haven't been . . . all together. I'm having to learn to do things . . . that I've never . . . things that Jack always took care of. I just hope I didn't do something wrong. *(Pause)* A lot of changes. Yeah, definitely a lot of changes. *(To the* GIRL*)* Right, honey? But we're the two musketeers. We'll make it through. I'm trying to just . . . put my life back together. *(Pause)* A few things . . . some pictures *(tears starting to well up in her eyes)* . . . I really hate to lose the pictures. You know, of . . . Jenny when she was a baby, Mom and Dad, Jack and me when things were . . . better. Actually, I think I cut up most of those. But the pictures . . . those are the things you can't get back . . . you know? *(Pause)* And I lost my Bible. It was Mama's. She had . . . all our birthdays, my brothers and mine, when we were married . . . her favorite verses underlined. I can't get that back. Oh . . . wow . . . *(Starting to get emotional)* I gotta stop talking about things . . . I'll start to really cry. When I cry . . . I really cry. Not tonight . . . tonight I'm thankful . . . tonight I have my little girl. Tonight I'm not going to think about what I don't have . . . what's in *(turning back over her shoulder)* there. I'm going to be thankful. *(Hugs her little* GIRL; *pause)* About a month ago . . . right after the divorce was final. Jack and I have tried to be friends. I want Jenny to have both of us . . . as much as we can. Tomorrow is his day. I guess I'll have to give him a call and tell him. Maybe he can pick Jenny up earlier than we'd planned. *(Pause)* I can call my church too. It's across town, but . . . there are a lot of really good people there. I just joined two weeks ago. *(Pause)* Yeah, I was raised in the church . . . I just sort of drifted away. I guess I'm like any kid . . . I thought I could control everything. You think that when you're

33

young, but you can't. Things aren't always as they seem. I wish I could do most of it over again, but it's like the Bible in the house . . . *(Motioning to where her house once stood)* . . . there are some things you can't get back again. Mama kept praying for me. I'd call her on the phone, and she'd say, "I'm praying, honey." I dismissed it at the time, but as things went along in my marriage . . . every time I'd talk to her, I waited to hear her say it. It was hope, you know. Something I could hold on to. *(Pause)* No. She passed away four months ago . . . right before Christmas. I got her Bible. It's all I really wanted. When I opened it up . . . on the inside page, right beside my name and birth date it said, "Pray." *(Looking up)* It worked Mama. *(Pause)* I started going back to church a few weeks ago . . . really good people. Not how I remember church. I've started to think about some of the things I learned when I was a kid. About how Jesus loves me . . . *(Beat)* I feel good . . . when I'm there. I feel hope. It's such a gift to feel hope again, you know. To know that everything is gonna be OK *(Pause)* Tomorrow's Easter, huh?

FIREMAN *(handing her a large Bible):* Ma'am, we found this.

MOTHER *(in disbelief):* Mama's Bible! You found Mama's Bible! *(To her daughter)* Look, Jenny! *(To the* FIREMAN*)* Oh, thank you. Thank you! (FIREMAN *exits. She looks at it and holds it close. To the person.)* Miracles do happen! I can't believe it. *(Pause)* Thank you. We'll be OK. Have a Happy Easter. *(To the sky)* Everything's gonna be OK.

Guess Who's Coming to Dinner

Performance Tips and Pointers: This is a comedy sketch to use early on in your Christmas program. It is a "slice of life" piece that reminds us of something we can all identify with—relatives coming for the holidays. The set can be as simple or as elaborate as you want. A suggestion would be to put a couch with a table or two chairs on stage left and the Christmas tree stage right. Entrance from the kitchen would be stage left. (It could be reversed, naturally—whatever gives the characters plenty of stage to cross on entrances and exits.) A musical suggestion would be opening the piece with an up-tempo instrumental bump of "Have Yourself a Merry Little Christmas.") Approximate running time: 8 minutes.

Topic: Having relatives over for the Christmas dinner

Scripture: None that we can find, but it's still a good sketch

Set: Middle-class family living room. (Optional) Two chairs, couch, end table, Christmas tree, doorbell.

Time: Early to mid-afternoon

Characters:
CRAIG: *a man in his 30s dressed in slacks, a long-sleeve shirt with his sleeves rolled up, and suspenders. He is a kid in a grown-up body. The idea of his in-laws coming over both scares and amuses him.*

LISA: *his humorous and ever-optimistic wife. She firmly believes that "Christmas is a family time." She enjoys the child in her husband but knows how to pull him into adulthood at the right time.*

TRENT: *their 8-year-old son (could be as old as 11, if need be); doing anything to get out of the house. He's got a quick wit, much like his mother's.*

Synopsis: It is Christmas and Craig's in-laws are coming over for dinner. In-laws are bad enough, but these relatives are straight out of *One Flew Over the Cuckoo's Nest*. Lisa knows they are a little strange, but "Christmas is a family time." In this family, Halloween would be more appropriate.

(Scene opens with CRAIG *sneaking into the living room. He looks around and then makes a beeline to the Christmas tree. He immediately starts looking at all the packages, hoping to find one with his name on it.)*

CRAIG: Lisa—Trent—*(Noticing his gift)* Ah-ha! Craig.

(He picks it up and shakes it; then we hear what sounds like a doll say "mama.")

LISA *(offstage):* Craig!

CRAIG *(about drops the gift and says with a terrified tone):* What? *(Getting his composure)* Honey.

LISA *(offstage):* I need some help with the turkey.

CRAIG: Oh—which one of your relatives is in the kitchen, dear?

LISA *(offstage):* Very amusing, sweetheart. Now put the gift down and get your partially balding head in the kitchen.

CRAIG: You've got a sadistic streak, Lisa. It's not particularly attractive at Christmas. What makes you think I was looking at gifts?

*(*TRENT *enters.)*

TRENT: Dad, can I go over to Randall's?

CRAIG: Now? But your Aunt Louise and the rest of Mom's family are going to be here any minute.

TRENT: I know. Don't tell Mom—but they're weird.

CRAIG: She knows they're weird, Son—but they're family. Christmas is a time for family—even if they are rejects from a Loony Tunes cartoon. *(Imitating Porky Pig)* A-b-b . . . That's all folks!

(They both start to laugh as LISA *enters.)*

LISA: What's going on out here?

CRAIG: Oh . . . nothing . . . just talking about . . . life.

LISA: Life, huh? You were making fun of my relatives.

CRAIG: No . . . sweetheart . . . *(Changing subjects)* Say, didn't you need help with the turkey?

LISA *(pops his suspenders):* He's beyond help.

CRAIG: Ow!

TRENT: No offense, Mom—but why did we have to have *(looking at* LISA *cautiously)* them over on Christmas?

LISA: Them, meaning your aunts and uncles who love you as if you were their own son?

TRENT *(guilty):* Yeah.

LISA: Because . . . Christmas is *(everyone—*LISA, CRAIG, *and* TRENT*—say it together)* a family time. OK, you two. It is . . . It's a time to share.

TRENT: But they make me . . . they're scary.

LISA: So, we'll all be scared together.

CRAIG *(evil):* Ho, ho, ho.

TRENT: Couldn't we just send 'em a fruitcake instead?

LISA: Trent.

TRENT: Well, instead of Christmas . . . how about Halloween?

CRAIG: It does seem more appropriate.

LISA: Come on—it's just for a few hours. How bad can that be?

(At that point both CRAIG *and* TRENT *do a slow pan to* LISA.*)*

LISA: They are not that bad.

CRAIG: Sweetheart, the last time your family was here, I had to stand guard on the porch just to keep all the neighborhood kids away.

LISA: You know, that's right; I never did understand what all those kids wanted.

CRAIG: They thought the circus was in town!

*(*TRENT *makes a monkey noise and jumps around.)*

LISA: OK, funny men. They are a little different, but they are a part of me— flesh of my flesh, bone of my bone.

CRAIG: Honey, they are definitely from the shallow end of your gene pool.

TRENT: Mom—last year, Aunt Louise kissed me so many times I thought I had permanent drool marks.

LISA: She loves you.

TRENT: So, tell her to wave at me instead. It was embarrassing.

LISA: I'll do what I can.

TRENT: And Aunt Mertie isn't going to make me hold her teeth again, is she?

LISA: You had to hold Aunt Mertie's teeth?

TRENT: She kept saying—if I concentrated hard enough, they would talk on their own.

CRAIG: Did they?

TRENT: Dad! *(They laugh.)*

LISA: They're going to be here any minute—just be nice—

CRAIG *(interrupting):* Keep a towel handy. *(Nudges* TRENT)

LISA: And it'll be over with before you know it.

CRAIG: That's what they told me when I had that root canal.

LISA: Oh—and you'll be sitting by Cousin Ernest.

CRAIG *(terrified):* No! Not Cousin Ernest! Anyone but Cousin Ernest! That man—that man can crack walnuts with his eyebrows. When he breathes, his nose hairs blow in and out like little squids. I can't eat next to that man. I know—Trent, I'll take Aunt Louise.

TRENT: No way, Dad. I'll sit on Aunt Louise's lap with Aunt Mertie's teeth on my plate before you stick me with Cousin Ernest.

CRAIG: Honey, what did I do? How did I mistreat you that you want me to suffer dinner next to this man?

LISA *(interrupting):* Craig! He's a nice man. A retired pastor.

CRAIG: He's a crazy man. He used to yell at the end of the service, "Elvis is leaving the building!"

LISA: So, he's a little eccentric.

CRAIG: He showed up last year with his underwear on the outside of his pants.

(At this point the doorbell rings. CRAIG *and* TRENT *look up terrified.)*

LISA: They're here. Now, on our best behavior. It's Christmas—a family time.

*(*CRAIG *reaches over and hands* TRENT *a dish towel.* LISA *walks to the door, opens it, and we hear from offstage . . .)*

OFFSTAGE VOICE: Elvis is entering the building!

*(*CRAIG *and* TRENT *look at each other with horror on their faces.)*

Blackout

Fossils

Performance Tips and Pointers: This is not an easy scene to stage or act, but it is very effective. The swivel chair should have a high back so when Fred turns his back, it covers him and he can change his look. Fred, at the beginning, should be a wiser and more subdued individual; then when he is 20 years younger, we see his more stubborn, aggressive side. The scene between the Son and Fred should be filled with long, awkward pauses. Don't rush the scene. There is a lot of ground that is between the lines. It is filled with thought. Approximate running time: 10 to 12 minutes.

Topic: Forgiveness, taking the opportunities when they're there

Scripture: Ephesians 4:32

Set: Living room. A swivel chair, end table and lamp, papers, coats, shirt.

Time: Evening

Characters:
> FRED: *(beginning/end) a man in his late 60s (during the middle) 20 years younger*
> HARRIET: *his patient and physical wife*
> STEVE: *their son, who left 2 years ago angry*
> SUE: *Steve's new wife*

Good for Sermons On: Forgiveness ● Why did Christ come into the world? ● Taking advantage of the moments we have

Synopsis: Fred is struggling with things he never said to his son when he had the chance. Steve left two years ago over a fight he and his father had. He hasn't seen his parents since then. But today, Thanksgiving, he's coming home to introduce his wife and say "I'm sorry—and I love you." The scene is done in flashbacks through the eyes of Fred.

(Scene opens with a fairly tight spot on an elderly man in a swivel lounge chair. Next to the chair is an end table and lamp.)

FRED: Ever stop to think about this time of year much? Yeah, yeah, yeah, I know. Everybody knows about Thanksgiving. Family gatherings, big meals, indigestion, and Christmas right around the corner. But I'm not talking about that. I'm talking about how . . . I mean Thanksgiving now, by which I mean today, should be more than we tend to make it. Think about it. In my eyes, it's a time to look back on the past year, good or bad, with a sense of gratitude, you know *(looks up)*, thank You. *(Looks back to audience)* Then it's on to Christmas with its new birth, its hope for a new beginning, a new . . . life, and there it is, and then the New Year sneaks up, sorta like an afterthought. You see, you see, all connected, that's how I see it, but all too easily we seem to lose that somehow. It's still a pretty package, mind you, but under the paper and ribbon is—more paper, I guess. That and the old bones of memories of all your past Thanksgivings and Christmases that didn't have the real . . . purpose they were supposed to. Am I making myself clear, I talk in circles sometimes. *(Beat)* But for some folks, that's all they've got— I'm back to the old bones part, tell ya what, we'll call 'em fossils—not that remembering old family holidays is a negative. No, no, I've got my own share of fossils that rattle around me at this time of year, good and bad. But that's my meaning really. At one point in my life, that's all I had. Not that I cared. But I hadn't learned yet. You live, you learn. You see, like it or not, fossils can have teeth. Do you see? *(Quietly)* They can eat you alive.

(Lights come up on the set behind FRED. *Set consists of a sofa, throw rug, coffee table, and a door leading into the kitchen.* HARRIET, *a 40-year-old woman,* FRED's *wife, enters carrying a freshly pressed shirt.)*

HARRIET: Fred! *(*FRED *turns in his swivel chair and turns his back to us.)* Look at this place! It's a disaster area. You've scattered your newspaper everywhere. *(All we see of* FRED *is the back of his chair as* HARRIET *continues.)* And look at you. You look as bad as this room. Here, put on this shirt. I swannee. If you sit here in this squalor while Steve brings his new bride in here, you'll scare her half to death.

*(*FRED *stands; he's now dressed in a T-shirt, maybe a ball cap, and we see, even from the back, that he's now about 20 years younger.)*

FRED: Now hold on there, Harriet! I think you're putting the cart before the horse here. This is my house we're standing in here, huh? If I want to be comfortable in my own house, then I'll . . . and besides that, I'm sure he's already told her enough horror stories about his old man to fully prepare her for me in a T-shirt.

HARRIET: Our house.

FRED: What?

HARRIET: This is our house.

FRED: Oh, yeah, sure it is. I'm just . . . you know.

HARRIET: Fred, he's been out of our lives for almost two years now. This is an important overture he's making here. I want him to be as comfortable as pos- . . .

FRED *(interrupting):* And that!

HARRIET: What?

FRED: Just because Stevie storms out of here in a huff and decides he's going to cut his family out of his life for two years doesn't mean I'm supposed to drop to my knees and genuflect when he deigns to give us his attention again, bride or no.

HARRIET: Don't do this, Fred. These past two years have been very difficult for me. And you know that you're every bit as much to blame for this as he was.

FRED: Wha? Me?

HARRIET: Fred! I want this to be a good Thanksgiving together. And if you do anything to ruin it . . . *(She looks at him with the full intent of what will happen if he spoils things.)* Don't! Please.

FRED: Fine, fine, fine.

HARRIET: Put on this shirt. *(She tosses it to him.)*

FRED: Fine. *(The doorbell rings.)* I'll get it.

HARRIET: No! I'll answer the door. Just clean up the paper . . . please.

FRED: Fine. (HARRIET *exits while* FRED *cleans and grumbles.* STEVE, SUE, *and* HARRIET *enter smiling, coats in hand.)*

FRED: Don't put 'em on the couch. Der Fuehrer, here, will have you cleaning the place with a toothbrush.

STEVE: Huh?

HARRIET: Fred. *(To them)* Don't mind him. *(Crosses to* FRED) He's just a little blustery today. *(Pinches* FRED's *cheek)*

FRED: Ow!

HARRIET: We're both so happy to have you here. Here, let me take your coats.

SUE: Thank you. (HARRIET *exits with coats.)*

(Awkward pause)

STEVE: Uh . . .

FRED: Back to face the music, huh?

STEVE: What?

FRED: Grab the bull by the horns—come in out of the rain. Well, don't worry, Son. I won't bite ya. I won't even bring up your past actions. I'm sure you're older and wiser by now. *(Shakes STEVE's hand)* So, who's this beautiful lady you've brought with you?

STEVE *(taken aback by his father's statements):* Uh . . .

SUE: I'm Sue. *(She extends her hand.)* Steve told me so much about you.

FRED *(takes her hand and bends to kiss it):* I'm sure he has. (HARRIET *comes back in.)* I'm also sure that you're surprised that I don't have one eye and drag my knuckles when I walk too.

HARRIET *(slaps FRED on the bottom):* Fred!

FRED *(responding):* Ieeeye!

HARRIET: Fred likes to be so playful. *(Takes him by the ear)* Don't you, dear?

FRED *(in obvious pain):* Yeah, yeah. I'm a regular Milton Berle. *(She releases him.)*

HARRIET: You look lovely in that dress, Sue. The color is beautiful.

SUE: Why, thank you. Steve bought it for me. He knows where I like to shop. In fact, that's where we first met. He was buying something for his girlfriend, and he asked me if I liked the style. Then one thing just led to another.

FRED: A bird in hand, huh, Steve? (HARRIET *elbows him.)* Oooof!

HARRIET: Sue, I've got a few things to do before dinner. Why don't we use that time to get to know each other a bit. We can leave these two on their own. I'm sure they won't get into trouble. *(This last line is delivered to FRED with just the right look. FRED, still gasping, raises his hands in a gesture of peace and surrender. The ladies exit. FRED sits down during another awkward pause.)*

STEVE: You and Mom seem to be getting along pretty well.

FRED: Yeah. I just gotta keep her away from that Championship Wrestling.

STEVE *(beat):* It's uh . . . good to see you.

FRED: Is it?

STEVE *(pause):* How do you like Sue?

FRED *(stares at STEVE):* Pretty.

STEVE *(long pause):* Happy Thanksgiving.

FRED: Oh yeah.

STEVE *(sighs):* Look, Dad . . . I don't know what to say.

FRED *(takes control):* All right. *(Stands while glaring at* STEVE) So what do you want here, Son? What exactly did you expect? You want me to forgive and forget? Or did you think I'd say it was all my fault? *(Affected voice)* "Please, Sonny boy, come back home." You go running off without word one. Your mother's worried half to death. Do we get a letter? A postcard maybe? A note in a bottle? Two years. You see, see? Four months ago we hear, hear mind you, from some overfed busybody at the hair salon, that you got married. Not one call. Not one invite. You mother cries herself to sleep. You know what that sounds like? You don't know . . . *(Controls himself before he uses language he'll regret)* Then, bam! Out of the blue you call. Seems you and Sue have got religion now. Hoo-wah. So now, here you are at my doorstep, saying you don't know what to say. I'd think that after two years, you could have saved up a book full of things to say. How about how rotten the old man is. You got that chapter ready? So, you got the inside track with God. He must help you see just what a lousy dad I am? Especially on those long, cold nights when you're reading the Good Book. Come on, spill it, boy. Pile it on me.

STEVE: That's . . . that's not it.

FRED: Well, I'm waiting.

STEVE *(reaching for some solid ground):* Wait, wait. This has all been really stupid. (FRED *rears up to respond, but* STEVE *hurries ahead.)* And it's been my fault. I don't know where all the fights between you and me started, and I don't really care right now.

FRED: Yeah, well . . .

STEVE: I know there's been a lot of pain spread around here. My leaving, no communication. I used to have this litany of reasons. But that's gone now. I blame myself . . . a hundred ways. But I . . . *(Pause)* OK. Look. I'm sorry. I'm sorry about all that with Mom. She was sort of just in the middle, but I didn't think about how it'd all hurt her so much. And then with you . . . *(Looks at his dad for a moment)* I'm sorry. Sincerely sorry.

FRED: That's pretty. That what you came to say?

STEVE: No. Well, yes. But there's something else too. *(Sighs)* I had this whole speech thing all planned out. A page and a half at least. It seems so stupid now. Let me just say this. This . . . this whole time of year is important. I mean it celebrates God's grace to us. I mean Thanksgiving, you know, giving thanks. Then there's Jesus' birth at Christmas. Look, Dad, if any of this celebrating holidays stuff means anything, I think it's supposed to be forgiveness—love enough to forgive. It took me a few Thanksgivings to finally realize that. *(Beat)* I forgive you, Dad—and I want you to forgive me. *(Beat)* I—I love you. That's what's important to me now. I love you.

(Very long pause as FRED *looks at his son.* FRED *battles with his inner emotions.)*

FRED: Uh . . .

(HARRIET *and* SUE *enter.*)

HARRIET: Well, boys, dinner's ready. Let's eat.

FRED *(clears throat):* Yeah . . . yeah. Let's chow down.

HARRIET: Everything all right? Something wrong, Fred . . . Steve?

FRED *(moving to his lounge chair, he sits with his back to the audience):* Nah . . . no, you guys go ahead—I'll be right in.

(HARRIET, SUE, *and* STEVE *move to exit. Before* STEVE *goes through the door, he stops and looks back at his dad. After a brief pause, there is no response, so* STEVE *exits. The set lights begin to fade except for a spot on* FRED's *chair, which is still turned away from the audience. The lamp light is on.* FRED *swivels back to the audience, and he's aged again.*)

FRED: That one had its teeth in me for some time. I kept seeing my son standing in that doorway with his eyes searching me for a word, any word. He kept lookin' at me as if I had it in my shirt pocket or something. He was forgiving me, passing me the peace pipe, opening the door. And I was the bullheaded fool that just sat there with his pockets empty, his jaw clamped tight, and his doors locked. *(Beat)* My kid was braver than I gave him credit for. I was the coward. *(Pause)* Anyway, he didn't make it back for Christmas. Never made it back for anything after that. In fact, the last time I saw my son . . . *(pause as he stops himself from choking up)* saw my . . . son alive, was that night. Now, his death wasn't something dramatic or, or, sudden, but it might as well have been, for all my pigheadedness. Foolish. *(From this point on the spot on* FRED *begins to fade until he is partially lit only by the lamp on the end table.)* But you see? My point here is, my boy opened more than one door for me that night. One I left closed. To my own loss. Praise be, eventually I walked through the second. You grieve, you learn. You catching my meaning? Thanksgiving can be a much more meaningful time than we give it credit for. It doesn't have to just be about old fossils. It comes down to us taking the time to make the right choices. But time can be a slippery thing if we don't keep track of it. You see, a few seconds from now is the future, then it becomes the present . . . *(FRED* leans forward *into the lamplight and reaches for the switch)* then it's . . . past.

Blackout

44

AND OTHER SPIRITUAL MATTERS

What Is a Christian?

Performance Tips and Pointers: These are a series of interviews to be used singly or together in a service or perhaps a youth event that asks the question: What is a Christian? Each scene should start with a musical tag that is the same every time. It sets in the audience's mind what is coming. Each scene could be enhanced with sound effects, such as street sounds, traffic, lunchroom, and so forth. Also, each scene should end with a quick blackout. The most difficult scene is Scene 1 because of the BLEEPS. This should be done by the actor saying the word "bleep" with possibly a sound at the same time. Be careful, some churches will have a hard time with the illusion that this person is saying "swear words."

Running time: 1—one minute, 2—one minute, 3—two minutes.

Topic: What is a Christian?

Scripture: Matthew 10:32; 1 John 4:4-5

Set: 1 and 2 on the street; 3 is in a lunchroom

Time: Anytime

Characters:
INTERVIEWER: *a typical on-the-street reporter*
YOUNG MAN: *a very demonstrative man with a foul mouth*
BOY: *a young man with air for a brain; should be played very dumb*
GIRL: *a high school student very embarrassed by the thought of being identified as a Christian*

Good for Sermons On: What is a Christian? ● People's perceptions of a Christian ● Standing up for Christ

Synopsis: We have an on-the-street interviewer asking people, "What is a Christian?" We get three different responses.

Interview 1

INTERVIEWER: Good evening, ladies and gentlemen. This is your on-the-street interviewer asking people everywhere the question: What is a Christian? Here's someone now. Excuse me, sir!

YOUNG MAN: Whoa *bleep!* What the *bleep* do you think you're doing. You sneak up on me like some *bleeping bleep*—and scare me half to death. Why I ought'a take that *bleeping* microphone and stick it in your *bleep!*

INTERVIEWER: I'm sorry, sir, . . . er . . . uh . . . but you can't . . . that is, I was just going to . . .

YOUNG MAN: What? Spit it the *bleep* out already.

INTERVIEWER: Never mind, really. I'm sorry to bother you. I was just asking what people thought a Christian was . . .

YOUNG MAN: Oh. Well—I'm a Christian.

INTERVIEWER: You are?

YOUNG MAN: Sure. Didn't you see this cross I'm wearing? I wear it all the time. I even shower with it.

INTERVIEWER: Oh . . . well . . . thank you.

YOUNG MAN: Sure. No *bleeping* sweat, man. Oh and—God bless.

Interview 2

INTERVIEWER: This is your on-the-street interviewer asking people everywhere . . . oh, wait, here's a fine example of today's youth. I'll approach him with our question. Excuse me, young man.

BOY: Wha?

INTERVIEWER: I'd like to ask you a question.

BOY: Oh, uh-huh, sure, cool.

INTERVIEWER: What is a Christian?

BOY: Uh huh?

INTERVIEWER: Well, what do you think?

BOY: Cool.

INTERVIEWER: No, I mean I'm asking you. What is a Christian?

BOY: Oh, oh! OK, yeah . . . uhmm . . . ah . . . well it's like a person who . . . is like into God and stuff. Uh, I don't know. They like to tell you what to do and stuff. Oh! And they don't like to party, ya know? Like a little liquid refreshment, ya know! Uh . . . they're just . . . *stupid.*

INTERVIEWER: Really? Well, what makes them "stupid"?

BOY: Oh . . . uh . . . well it's just . . . I don't know.

INTERVIEWER: Well, thank you, sir.

BOY: Wha?

Interview 3

INTERVIEWER: Excuse me, miss.

GIRL: Huh?

INTERVIEWER: I'm an on-the-street interviewer asking people everywhere the question: What is a Christian?

GIRL: Shhh!

INTERVIEWER: What?

GIRL *(whispering):* Be quiet! Do you want everybody to hear you?

INTERVIEWER *(whispering):* Sorry. Is there a problem? Why are we whispering?

GIRL *(whispering):* Because, if they hear me talking to you, then they'll know I know and if they know I know, then they'll know I am and that's that!

INTERVIEWER *(whispering):* If they know you know, then they'll know you are and that's that?

GIRL *(whispering):* Yes.

INTERVIEWER *(whispering):* What are we talking about? Who are "they"?

GIRL *(whispering):* My friends . . . go away.

INTERVIEWER *(whispering):* No, wait. I don't understand what you're saying. They'll know you are what? Are you a Christian?

GIRL *(whispering):* Yes. Now go away.

INTERVIEWER *(full voice):* Wait, what's the problem?

GIRL *(whispering):* Shh. I know what a Christian is all right? And I know why it's important to be one. I go to church every Sunday, and it's all great. But—if my friends find out, then *I'm* out, all right? During the week, I'm just normal, I don't do anything bad, I just have fun with my friends, and I'm not giving that up.

INTERVIEWER *(whispering):* You think you have to give up your friends to be a Christian?

GIRL *(whispering):* I won't give *them* up; they'll give *me* up. If I did everything they tell me at church, like hand out tracts, quote all the time from the Bible, and drag all my friends to youth meetings, then everybody'd drop me like a hot rock!

INTERVIEWER *(whispering):* But, doing all those things, is that really what being a Christian is all about?

GIRL *(pause, whispering):* I don't know. I'm leaving now. Good-bye.

INTERVIEWER: Good-bye. This is your on-the-street interviewer signing off.

What's Next?

Performance Tips and Pointers: This is a readers theatre piece primarily for youth but can be done by any age. It can be done in a number of ways (i.e., in a straight line or with Reader 3 in front and all the other Readers on small blocks behind Reader 3). The key is the expression in each of the Readers' voices. When you see "Characters" in parentheses, they should be broad. The key is to keep the pace moving. Approximate running time: 6 to 7 minutes.

Topic: After we become a Christian, then what do we do?

Scripture: Mark 12:29-31

Set: Simple, straight line or using blocks to stand on

Time: Anytime

Characters:
READER 3: *main character asking the questions*
READERS 1, 2, and 4: *playing all the other parts*

Good for Sermons On: What does being a Christian mean? • Now I'm a Christian, what next? • The Christian life

Synopsis: Reader 3 is asking the question, "Now that I'm a Christian, what's next?" Readers 1-4: A readers theatre examination of what's next?

READER 1: I'm a Christian now, so what's next?

READER 2: What's next?

READER 3: OK, so I understand pretty well about salvation, you know—but my friend said it was all emotion.

READER 4 *(friend):* Why do you get caught up in this stuff? It's all brainwashing. Just don't talk to me about it. I'm not gonna go drink grape Kool-Aid.

READER 3: I wasn't sure what he meant about the Kool-Aid, but I knew he was wrong about brainwashing. It was a choice. I understood God's sacrifice for me and I . . .

READERS 1, 2, 4: Made a choice.

READER 3: It was emotional, but more. Know what I mean?

READER 2: "For God so loved the world,

READER 4: that He gave His only begotten Son,

READER 1: that whoever believes in Him should not perish,

READER 1, 2, 4: but have eternal life." [John 3:16]

READER 3: Right. I've even started reading the Bible. At first it was sort of weird, you know. But it's starting to make sense.

READER 1: "The testimony of the LORD is sure, making wise the simple." [Psalm 19:7]

READER 3: Right—simple . . . Simple? Anyway, what I want to know now is . . .

ALL: What's *next?*

READER 3: Don't get me wrong. I'm not bored or anything. Well, maybe I am a little bored. (READER 4 *starts snoring.*) It's just . . . I want to be useful. I want to do something. What am I supposed to do?

READER 1: What am I supposed to be?

READER 3: Right.

READER 2 (*as a Southern pastor*): What is the will of God?

READER 3: Yeah . . . yeah . . . God's will. That's what I need. But *wait!* What if He wants me to be a . . .

READERS 1 and 2: Missionary!

READER 4 (*makes jungle noises all the way till the word "bugs"*)

READER 2 (*makes a Tarzan yell*)

READER 3: Whoa, please! I can't do that! Hacking through the undergrowth . . . living in a grass hut.

READER 1: Natives.

READER 2: Animals.

READERS 1 and 2: Bugs!

READER 3: I can't!

READERS 1, 2, and 4: Don't sweat the small stuff.

READER 3: Or maybe He wants me to be a . . . a . . . pastor.

READER 2 *(starts singing "Onward, Christian Soldiers")*

READER 3: But I can't do that either. I get all nervous whenever anybody just asks me to pray out loud. And if I even think about witnessing or handing out a tract . . . I get nosebleeds.

READERS 1, 2, and 4: Don't sweat the small stuff.

READER 3: Wait! Maybe I'm supposed to be a Christian artist.

READERS 1, 2, and 4 *(start applauding, while* READER 3 *bows, then an immediate cut-off)*

READER 2: A Christian what?

READERS 1, 2, and 4 *(start laughing till* READER 3 *cuts them off)*

READER 3: You know, a famous personality that sings . . . er, plays some instrument . . . or a . . . dances . . .

READERS 1, 2, and 4 *(start laughing again)*

READER 3: I can't do any of that stuff.

READERS 1, 2, and 4: Don't sweat the . . .

READER 3: Small stuff. Would you stop saying that, you stupid cows. If I can't do any of those things, what good am I to God?

READER 2 *(as the Southern pastor):* What's God's will?

READER 1: Teacher, which is the greatest commandment in the law?

READER 3: Huh?

READER 2 *(whispers in Southern drawl):* God's will.

READER 3: Oh yeah.

READER 2: And Jesus said to him.

READER 4: "You shall love the Lord your God with all your heart, and with all your soul, and with all your mind." [Mark 12:30]

READER 3: That's it? Just love God?

READER 2: *Love* God.

READER 3: Love . . . God?

READER 4: *Love* God.

READER 3: You mean—like real love? How do you do that with God? *(Searching)* I mean, if you really love somebody—you . . . wanna be with them.

READER 1: You wanna talk to them.

READER 3 *(getting into it):* Tell them how you feel.

READER 2: What's on your mind.

READER 4: "So I gave my attention to the Lord God, to seek Him by prayer and supplications . . ." [Daniel 9:3]

READER 3: Supplications?

READER 1 *(whispers):* Humble requests.

READER 2: Ooooo, you're smart.

READER 1: Thank you.

READER 3: So prayer is just like, uh . . . talking to God? Well, that's neat . . . No thees and thous and stuff? I think I can get the hang of that.

READER 4: "Worship the LORD with reverence, and rejoice with trembling." [Psalm 2:11]

READER 3: Oh yeah—that. But what does worship mean—really?

READER 1: Webster defines "worship" as

READER 2 *(stepping up on a block and becoming Webster):* "to regard with great or extravagant respect. To . . ."

READER 3 *(interrupting):* Well, at church they have a "worship time" and sing for about 40 minutes. But I don't even like the songs and junk. Does this mean I can't do this just 'cause I can't sing and stuff?

READER 2 *(as Webster, trying to get back his definition):* "To honor God."

READER 3: Honor God?

READER 2: Honor God.

READER 3: I don't have to sing to do that. I can honor God just about anytime—right?

READERS 1, 2, and 4: Right.

READER 3: Right. I'm on a roll now. *(Thinking)* Let's see, what else about love? Wait! What about hugs and stuff? I can't hug God. But that's part of love, isn't it?

READER 4: "A new commandment I give to you, that you love one another, even as I have loved you, that you also love one another." [John 13:34]

READER 3: Huh?

READER 2 *(whispers):* Fellowship.

READER 3: Oh. So you get your hugs from God through fellowship with other Christians?

READER 1: "And the King will answer and say to them,

READER 4 (as Jesus): 'Truly I say to you, to the extent that you did it to one of these brothers of Mine, even the least of them, you did it to Me.'" [Matthew 25:40]

READER 3: So I can serve God through others, and I can get a pat on the back or a kick in the butt.

READER 2 (kicks him in the butt)

READER 3 (a little annoyed at READER 2): If I need it, from them too? This is starting to make sense.

READERS 1, 2, and 4: Amen.

READER 3: But isn't that too simple? God's will is that I love Him? But what about all the other—stuff? What do I do? Who do I marry? Where am I gonna live? What about college?

READER 1: "Rejoice in the Lord always; again I will say . . ." [Philippians 4:4]

READER 3: Rejoice?

READER 4: Enjoy.

READER 2: Love God.

READER 1: Through prayer.

READER 2: Worship.

READER 4: Fellowship and service.

READER 3: And . . . enjoy. So that's what's next.

READER 4: That . . . and . . .

ALL: DON'T SWEAT THE SMALL STUFF.

Mac and Newt

Performance Tips and Pointers: This is a simple sketch that is very character driven. The two elderly gentlemen are close friends. That connection needs to be seen. I would start the scene with a short, tender musical intro, then if possible have a few car doors closing and cars pulling away. The lighting should be very warm. Running time: 5 minutes.

Topic: What can we expect in death?

Scripture: Matthew 7:24-17

Set: Very simple, two folding chairs center stage

Time: Anytime, but it might be more effective in the late afternoon

Characters:
MAC: *an elderly gentlemen in his 70s who is a little edgy; has a habit of biting his fingernails*
NEWT: *his friend, who is also in his 70s; soft-spoken and patient*

Good for Sermons On: Salvation ● What happens after we die ● How do we view God

Synopsis: A dear friend has died, and Mac and Newt are the last ones to leave the gravesite. Mac is very uncomfortable with hanging around. Newt on the other hand wants to sit and reminisce. The dynamics of the two gentlemen's personalities, coupled with the event that just took place, gives Newt a chance to talk to Mac about why he is uncomfortable with the issue of death.

(Scene begins with an elderly gentleman, dressed in a dark suit, sitting on a chair. He is looking at a hole in the ground. It is the gravesite of a departed friend. After awhile, another elderly gentleman comes up from behind.)

MAC: Let's go.

NEWT: I wanna stay here a little longer.

54

MAC: And do what? It's not like you're in Hawaii overlooking the beach. You're at a graveyard starin' at a hole, for cryin' out loud.

NEWT: I wanna think and say good-bye.

MAC: So say good-bye and do your thinking in the car.

NEWT: I'm gonna miss him. Making us laugh . . . Marty feeding the pigeons.

MAC: So . . . we'll have to carry on.

NEWT: I'm not that funny.

MAC: Then you can feed the pigeons. Let's go. This place gives me the creeps.

NEWT: You're certainly in a good mood today.

MAC: We just finished a funeral . . . what kind of mood would you expect me to be in? I hate funerals—especially when I know the person.

NEWT: But it's a part of life.

MAC: So are politicians, but I don't need the reminder.

NEWT: Marty looked natural, didn't he?

MAC: They had too much rouge on 'im. He looked like Joan Crawford in *Mildred Pierce*.

NEWT: But natural.

MAC: That's a stupid statement anyway. "He looked natural." Why do they always say that? It's stupid.

NEWT: I suppose it's better than saying, "He looked dead."

MAC: Well, don't say it when I . . .

NEWT: Go.

MAC: Whatever.

NEWT: So, what do you want me to say?

MAC: Well, first of all . . . I'm not plannin' on dying. But if by chance I do, say . . . *(thinking)* "he looked blue" . . . or "he looked stiff." Just don't say . . . *(rethinking)* better yet, have me cremated. Then you can say, "He looked dusty."

NEWT: Don't you think that'll offend?

MAC: Who, me? Nah, I'll be dead.

NEWT: No, anyone who's around.

MAC: Who cares. We're old—we can say those things and get away with it. But I ain't plannin' on dying.

NEWT: I don't guess anybody does, but it's a part of life.

MAC: Yeah, you've said that.

NEWT: Why are ya afraid of it so much, Mac?

MAC: Who said I was afraid? I'm not afraid. Who said I was afraid to . . . ?

NEWT (*finishing his sentence):* Die. See, you can't even finish the sentence.

MAC: I didn't need too. You knew what I was talking about.

NEWT: But you're afraid of it.

MAC: OK, Einstein . . . you're so smart. How do you know?

NEWT: 'Cause you're biting your fingernails. (MAC *is ready to bite his fingernails again just as* NEWT *says the line. He catches himself.)* You been biting your fingernails since they rushed Marty to the hospital on Tuesday.

MAC: It's just a habit. Just like you playin' the psychiatrist.

NEWT: You're eating yourself, Mac. You do it when you get uptight.

MAC: So, funerals make me uptight.

NEWT: But they happen. You can't get so uptight, Mac. At our age, they happen quite a bit. If you keep eating yourself, you're gonna be two foot tall by spring. What are you so uptight about, Mac?

MAC: Nothin'.

NEWT: Mac.

MAC: Nothin' I tell ya.

NEWT (*just looks at him)*

MAC (*reluctantly):* I don't know what's out there.

NEWT: Oh.

MAC: Don't start preachin' at me, Newt. I'm not in the mood for preachin'.

NEWT (*thinking):* We had this neighbor when I was a kid. Mr. . . . Mr. Claven. Old Man Claven, as we kids called him. We made up stories about how he was evil—did things to kids. No one dared cross that stone fence he had around his property. If you did—he would capture you, boil you in oil, whatever our imaginations could come up with. You know how kids can be. I was certain he was the meanest man in the whole world, even though I'd never said a word to him. I just watched him—on the other side of that fence weed his garden or whittle on this front porch. I'm not sure where all the rumors about him got started . . . but one thing I was certain about—if I ever crossed on the other side of that fence, I was a goner. One day, I was playing with one of my daddy's ropes in this old tree out front. I slipped and the rope wrapped around my waist, you see. It was so tight I couldn't breathe—I couldn't yell. Well, I was just about to meet my Maker when I felt these strong hands lift me up and loosen the rope. It was Old Man Claven. He—uh—saved my life. Took me over to his house. Laid me down on his couch and took care of me till my dad got in from the field. After that, I got to know him. Every day I crossed that stone fence. And you know what I found?

MAC: I could guess, but you're gonna tell me, right?

NEWT: I found he wasn't evil at all. He was just a nice elderly gentleman that was just a little shy was all. We became good friends.

MAC (looking at him): That certainly made my day. A funeral and a nice little tidbit from your life.

NEWT: The point is—the other side of the fence can look pretty ominous. And the Keeper of the house can either be a stranger or a friend. It's all up to us. Whether we get to know Him or whether we don't. Marty knew that.

MAC (figuring out the story was to make a spiritual point): I see. You slipped one in on me, didn't ya, Newt?

NEWT: What?

MAC: What? You know what—a sermon. Probably pretty proud of yourself, huh?

NEWT: Mac. We've had the discussion a hundred times.

MAC: Yeah—both you and Marty gangin' up on me.

NEWT: We weren't ganging. We were just . . . tryin' to pound a little truth into a very hard head.

MAC (thinking): Stranger or a friend, huh? (Pause) You probably made the story up. (Looks at him) I'll think about it.

NEWT: Good. Ready to go?

MAC: Wanna go, huh?

NEWT: Yeah. Let's go to the park and feed the pigeons in Marty's honor.

(They stand up and start to exit.)

MAC: Think they have pigeons in heaven?

NEWT: Nah . . . just angels, and I doubt if they'll eat out of his hand.

Blackout

Who Is God?

Performance Tips and Pointers: This is a series of on-the-street interviews. They can be done back to back. Or you can space them throughout your service, leading up to the sermon. It is important to do the final piece (Scene 4). It would be good to start each piece with the same theme music and then bring the light up on the character. Running time: 1 to 2 minutes each.

Topic: Who is God?

Scripture: Psalm 18:31

Set:
Scene 1—in an elementary classroom of a public school. You will definitely need sound effects of guns and heavy artillery. Also, a desk and papers.
Scene 2—in a mall. You will need mall sound effects.
Scene 3—in a Laundromat. You will need a chair and a ladies magazine, possibly a laundry basket and a box of soap.
Scene 4—in the parking lot of a grocery store. You will need a bag of groceries and a wheelchair.

Time: All scenes take place during the day.

Characters:
Scene 1—TEACHER: *in her late 50s; very politically correct*
Scene 2—BOY: *a teenager dressed in the style of the day*
Scene 3—MAN: *in his 30s or 40s; blunt and to the point*
Scene 4—GIRL: *about 6*
WOMAN: *in her 30s; confined to a wheelchair*

Good for Sermons On: Who is God? ● Concepts of God

Synopsis: Four separate scenes that ask the question, "What do you think of God?"
Scene 1: God is politically incorrect, but we desperately need Him.
Scene 2: God is a character in a movie.
Scene 3: God is a slot machine, a "get rich scheme."
Scene 4: God is God.

Scene 1

(Scene opens in a school room: a TEACHER *is sitting at her desk looking over papers.)*

V.O.: Excuse me!

TEACHER *(looking up, she screams and dives under her desk, then slightly and slowly peeks over the top):* Sorry. *(Getting herself up, dusting herself off, and getting her composure)* I thought you were a child with a very large gun. You know these days, you have to be quick. You never know. *(Looks around as she says that)* I have six years left until my retirement, and I figure if I can hold on . . .

V.O.: We're doing random interviews, and we would like to know, "What do you think of God?"

TEACHER *(quickly looks around):* Shhhhhhhhhhhh! I don't think you can ask that question here. You know, separation of church and state. *(Coming up with a quick idea)* I know—let's just call Him "balloons." That way we'll know what we're talking about, but it won't violate any rules. Only six more years on my contract, you know. *(Thinking)* "Balloons" *(she winks)* is good. Definitely "a cut above." *(She laughs.)* A little humor. Goals 2000 stresses humor. Makes the "independently open charges" feel good about themselves.

V.O.: But what do you think of . . . ?

TEACHER *(interrupting as if to catch him):* Ah-ah! Balloons? Well, very little humor. You know, thou shalt not this—thou shalt not that. Needs to loosen up. Get a hipper image. I think "balloons" could be useful—you know, in preparing our kids for the 21st century. Don't you think. *(Bell sounds)* Oh, here come the little tykes now. *(We hear battle sounds, guns, heavy artillery as we go to a quick blackout.)*

Scene 2

(Scene takes place in a mall. Young BOY *is dressed in grunge. He is slouching. PLEASE FEEL FREE TO CHANGE DIALOGUE TO FIT A TEENAGER'S CONSTANTLY CHANGING SLANG.)*

V.O.: Excuse me, young man.

BOY: Oh wow! Like cool. Hey, is this like a movie or one of them television shows? You know, *A Hard Affair* or *20 Minutes.* Hey, where's that old guy that looks like a bulldog? You know the old one that—that asks the hard questions. Not a good day when you see that face.

V.O.: Excuse me, young man, but we're doing random interviews and asking people, "What do you think of God?"

BOY: What? Throw it up again, man. The mall's noisy. *(He yells.)* Hey, shut up! *(Mall sounds stop.)* Guy's trying to ask me a question. Sorry, sometimes people are rude, ya know.

V.O.: What do you think of God?

BOY: Well, I liked Him in *Raiders of the Lost Ark,* you know? Did you see it . . . you know when He melted all those people in the end. Really gross, man . . . but cool. Does He do that a lot?

V.O.: What?

BOY: Melt people. I got a few suggestions if He does. You know if He's like bored or something and needs something to do. Did I answer your question? (*Looking around as if the camera crew is leaving*) Mr.? Oh well . . . hang loose.

(Blackout)

Scene 3

(Scene opens in a laundry. A MAN *is sitting in a chair wearing a torn pair of sweat pants and an undershirt. He is reading a ladies magazine.)*

V.O.: Excuse me, sir!

MAN *(slowly looking over paper):* Yeah, what can I do for you? (*Noticing camera*) Hey! Get that outta here. I sent the support check.

V.O.: Sir, we're taking random interviews and asking people, "What do you think of God?"

MAN: You're kidding?

V.O.: No, I don't think so.

MAN: I think He's a joke. Yeah, a cruel joke dumped on us by very cruel people.

V.O.: What do you mean.

MAN: OK. OK. I used to think He was real—but no more. See, I saw this TV guy, ya know. And he said God wanted to bless me. I said great! I'm ready to be blessed! Only thing was . . . I had to send him my money and in return God would give me back tenfold. I thought great! I send him a hundred—I get a thousand. I send him a thousand—I get ten thousand. Sorta like a really good chain letter, ya know. Only I don't gotta send it to anyone but just one. So I did. Whatta ya think happened? A truck full of George Washington's? A mansion on the beach? Zip, nada, down the porcelain throne. Not a dime. I'm broke. Look at me. I'm so poor I had to arm wrestle an 80-year-old lady just to get 50 cents to do the wash. God? . . . Hey, He owes me big.

(Blackout)

Scene 4

(Scene takes place in a parking lot of a grocery store and a WOMAN *is in a wheelchair. She is holding a bag of groceries. A* GIRL, *her daughter, is pushing her.)*

V.O.: Excuse me, ma'am.

WOMAN: Yes

V.O.: We're doing random interviews and we want to know, "What do you think of God?"

WOMAN: If you would have asked me this questions six months ago, I probably would have given you a different answer. Then He was vengeful, uncaring. I would have said He was unconcerned since He allowed a drunk driver to run a stop sign and take . . . take these. *(Rubbing her legs)* I couldn't take dance lessons with my daughter anymore. I had to have help to just . . . just be a mother. I hated Him. Nothing made sense . . . until she *(looking over to where her daughter just walked)* . . . she came into my room one particularly bad day with something she made in Vacation Bible School. It was a cardboard picture frame decorated with bits of macaroni that had been sprayed gold. Her picture was in the center. At the bottom written in Magic Marker was "I know God loves me because" then underneath that in my daughter's own writing was "I still have you." *(She is a little choked up.)* I still don't understand everything . . . but I know He loves me. You asked me who God is . . . *(Said deliberately as a statement)* God is. I trust that now.

(Blackout)